MW01594888

Unless otherwise indicated, all Scripture quotations are taken from the King James Version of the Bible.
The Wisdom Notes of Mike Murdock 3 / B-311
ISBN 10: 1-56394-450-2 / ISBN 13: 978-1-56394-450-5
Copyright © 2011 by **MIKE MURDOCK**
Publisher/Editor: Deborah Murdock Johnson
Published by The Wisdom Center · 4051 Denton Hwy. · Ft. Worth, Texas 76117
1-817-759-BOOK · 1-817-759-2665 · 1-817-759-0300
MikeMurdockBooks.com

www.twitter.com/DrMikeMurdock

1

AGING

I Never Envy...Youth.
They Never Know...
What Is Coming Next... :)
(We Do.)

Aging©

2 *A*ge Difference =
Perception Difference.
You Are 20,000 Experiences...
Behind.
Seeds For Indescribable *Stress*.

3 *A*ge...Does Not Make You *Seasoned*.

4 *R*emembering What I Learned
Yesterday Is...Becoming A Real Task.
:)
Aging Is...Forgetting *Faster*
Than You Are Learning.

5 *I*f You Have Reached 40 Years Old
Without Learning To Apologize...
I Would Classify You As
An *Imbecile*...Living On Mercy.

6 *65* Years Old...Where Will I Invest
My Life Next?
...In Those Who *Honor*.
...In Those Who *Pursue*.
...In Those Who *Change*.

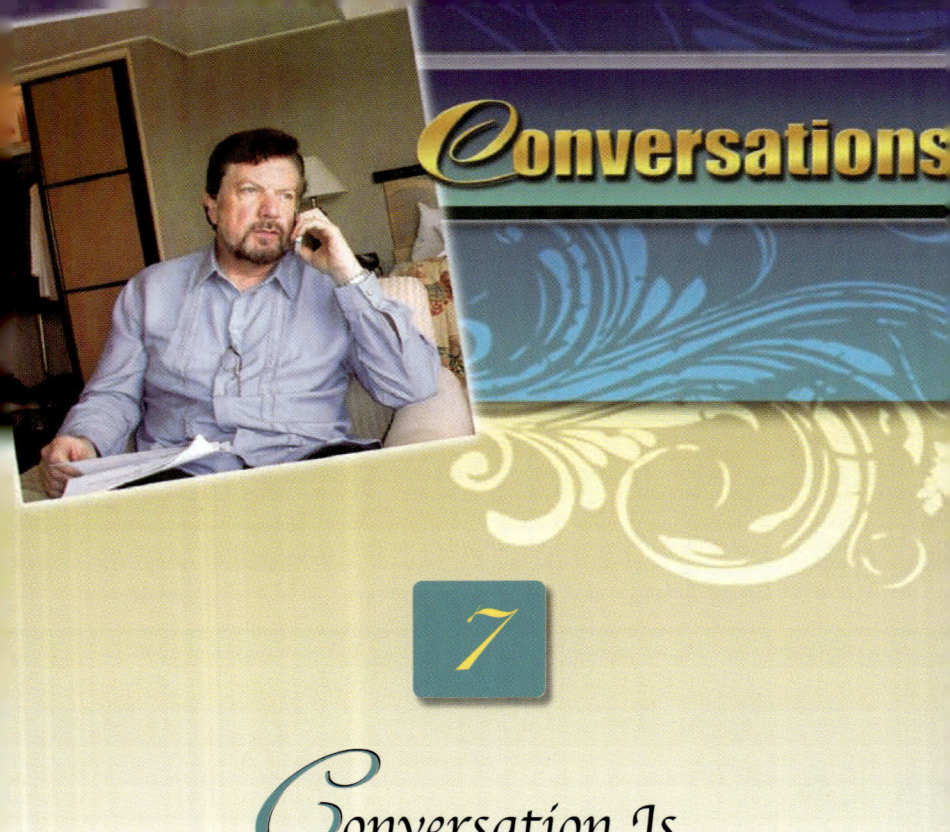

7

Conversation Is...
The Seed For Understanding.

Conversations

8 CONVERSATIONS Are...
Encyclopedias of Knowledge
...If You *Listen*.
...And, I Do.

9 Why Would I Desire
A Conversation With Someone...
Who Would Not Read My Books?
I *Wouldn't*.

10 Every CONVERSATION...
Needs A *Healer*.

11 Defective CONVERSATION Is...
The Reason Anything Fails.
Anything.

12 I Could Easily Become *Addicted*
To *Meaningful* Conversation...
If It Happened *Often* Enough.
:)

13 Every CONVERSATION Is...
A Major Investment.
I *Scrutinize* The Profit
...And The Loss.
Always.

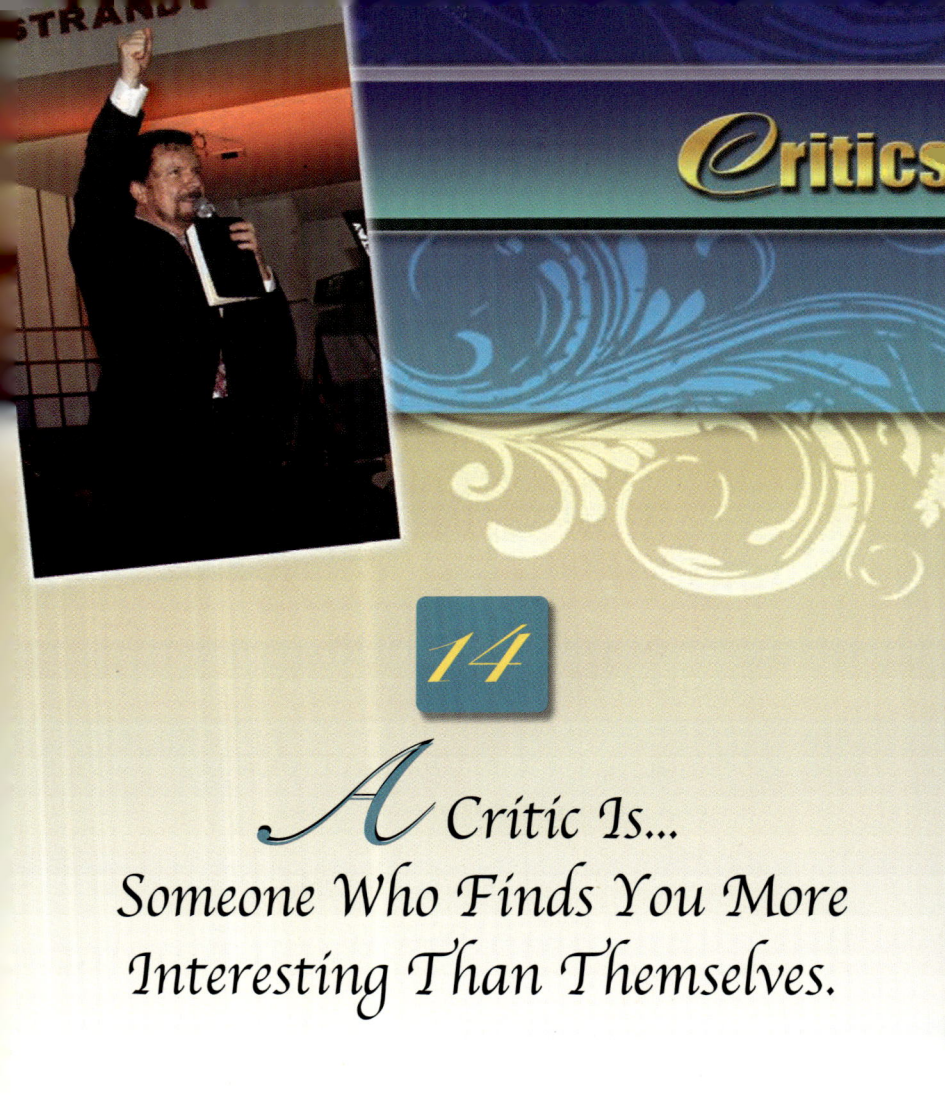

14

A Critic Is...
Someone Who Finds You More
Interesting Than Themselves.

Critics

15 CRITICS:
Him: "Have You Read What Your Critics Say?"
Me: "I Don't Research Opinions of... The Unlearned."
:) Smile.

16 CRITICS:
Criticism Hurts.
But, When You Study The Credibility of Your Critics...
All The Pain Goes Away.

17 CRITICS:
When You Are *Forced*
To Defend Yourself...
You Have Just Been Attacked.
Don't-Stay-Stupid.

18 CRITICS:
Judge Me.
It *Documents*...Your IQ.
:)

19 Your CRITICISM...Arrived,
Without The *Endorsement*
of Credibility.

20

Beauty...Gets A Man's Attention. Conversation...Keeps It.

Dad.

drMM

Do Not Miss A Single Message..!
~ drMMBlog.com ~

21 *R*eplace...Any *Machine*
That Does Not Work.
Replace...Any *Man*
That Does Not Work.
Dad.
drMM

22 *I*f You Want A Man To Remember
You...Do What *He* Wants.
If You Want A Man To Remember
You Longer...Do What He *Doesn't*
Want.
Dad.
drMM

23 *H*is Increased *Respect* Is...
Proof of His Increased Love.
Love Is...A Passion To *Please*.
Be-Smart.
Dad.
drMM

24 *W*hen He Hit You...He *Broke*
The Covenant.
Staying Does *Not* Reveal Your Love;
It Reveals Your Fear.
Dad.
drMM

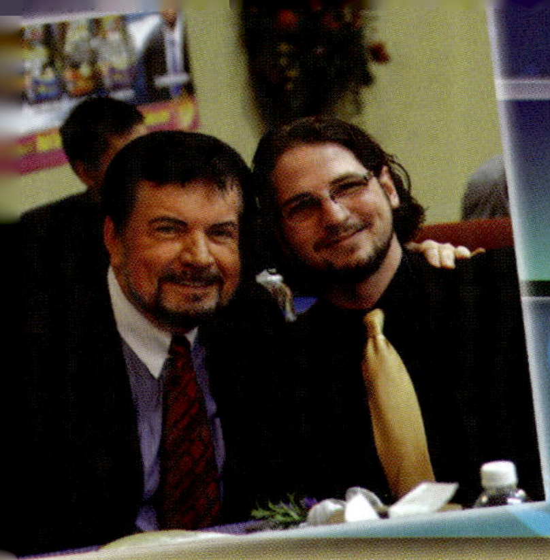

Dear Son

25

A Bitter Woman Is...
A Sad Experience...
And, No Man Can Cure Her.
(Only God.)
Dad.
drMM

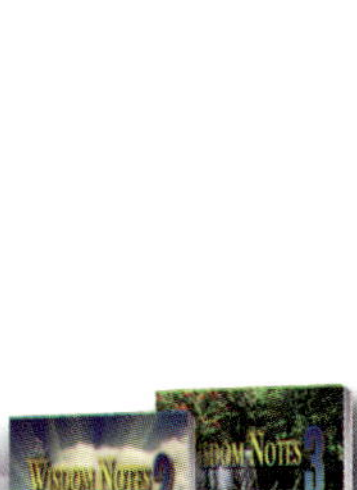

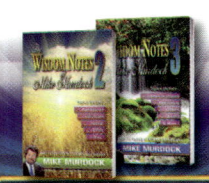

26 *R*uth Earned Credibility...
In His Fields Before She
Qualified...For His Name.
(Boaz/Marriage)
Dad.
drMM

27 *H*er Reque$t...Revealed Her
Perception of You.
...Money-Bags
...$ugar-Daddy
...Fool
Don't-Be-Stupid.
Dad.
drMM

28 *E*very Woman Is...*Different.*
The Woman Who Wants
$ponsorship Is...
Not Different *Enough.*
Dad.
drMM

29 *I*f She Does Not *Trust* Your
Decisions...She Will *Never* Feel *Safe.*
Dad.
drMM

Decisions

30

$\mathcal{S}$imple DECISIONS...
Create Instant Change.

*D*ecisions

31 *Y*our Decisions *Reveal* What You *Love*...or What You *Fear*.

32 *N*ever *Ignore* The DECISIONS of A *Rebel* In Your Environment.

33 *Y*our Goals...
Explain Your Decisions.
Your Decisions...
Reveal Your Mentors.
Your Mentorship...
Explains Your Wisdom.

34 *D*ESTINY Is...Simply *Wherever* Your Decisions *Bring* You.

35 *D*ECISIONS:
When You Have Asked *Enough* Questions...
Decision-Making Is *Easy*.
(Questions Are Doors To Knowledge.)

36 *Y*our Future Will *Arrive*...
At The *Speed* of Your Decisions.

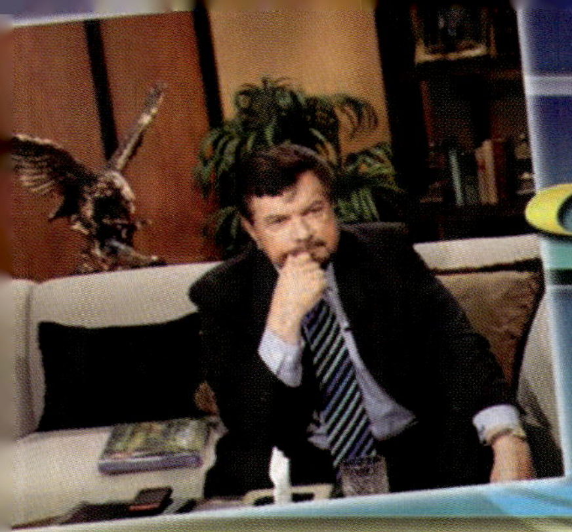

37

Eagles Discern Chickens Easily;
They Are The Ones...
Who Despise Eagles.
(Envy Is The Odor of...
The Intimidated.)

Eagle–Talk ©

38 Longest Recorded Flight
of A Chicken Is 13 *Seconds.*
But...They Can Give Advice
To Eagles...For *Hours.* :)

39 The Barnyard That *Thrills*
A Chicken...
Will *Kill* An Eagle.
Even Eagles...*Cannot* Improve
A Barnyard.

40 ONE HOUR With An Eagle Is...
Worth More Than A *Lifetime* With
A Chicken.
(Never Forget It.)

41 A True Eagle Is Not Arrogant;
Aloneness...*Cures* Arrogance.

42 The *Presence* of An Eagle...
Has Never *Excited* A Chicken.
Don't Expect It.
Just-FYI.

43 Your Patience...Does Not *Improve*
The Chicken.
Just-FYI.

44

*Fortunately For Us,
Fools Refuse To Hide.*

45 *A* Fool Is...Someone Who Makes The Same Mistakes *Repeatedly*. (Pro. 26:11)

46 *F*OOLS *Attempt* Withdrawals... Where They Have Never Made Deposits.

47 *L*OGIC Is...Always An *Unhappy* Experience For Fools.

48 *F*OOLS...Instruct *Upward*.

49 *K*INGLY-ANOINTING Is... Staying *Poised* In An Environment of Fools.

50 *F*OOLS Checklist:
Disdain...For Successful Achievers.
Dishonor...Toward Parents.
Defiance...Against Authority.

51 *O*nly A Fool *Ignores* Who The King Likes.

52 *F*OOLS...*Disdain*
The Environment of Favor.
(Absalom/Prodigal Son...
Look For Greener Grass.)
(Naomi To Ruth...Stay.)

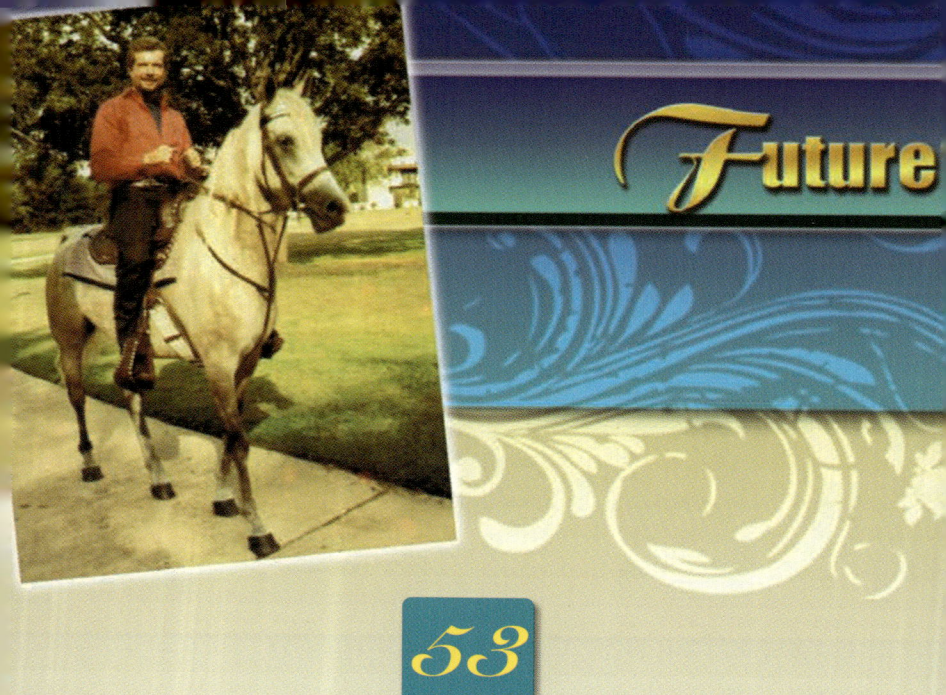

53

*W*hen I Know Who You Honor...
I Can Predict Your Future.

54 *Y*our *Potential* Is...
Not A *Prophecy* of Your Future.
Unrelated.
Completely.
(Lucifer/Absalom/Judas)

55 *T*he *Worst* Day In Your Future...
Will Be Greater Than The *Best* Day...
of Your Past.
"I Know The Plans I Have." ~God

56 *Y*our Reaction To An Instruction
Determines...Future Access.

57 *U*ntil You Can SEE Your Future...
You Will *Misinterpret* Every
Conversation God Has With You.

58 *T*he Price of Your Present Was...
Passion.
The Price of Your Future Is...
Credibility.

59 *W*hat Is..."The Future"...
You Are Training For?
WHO Is...Training You?
HOW...Are They Training You?
What Is...YOUR Investment?

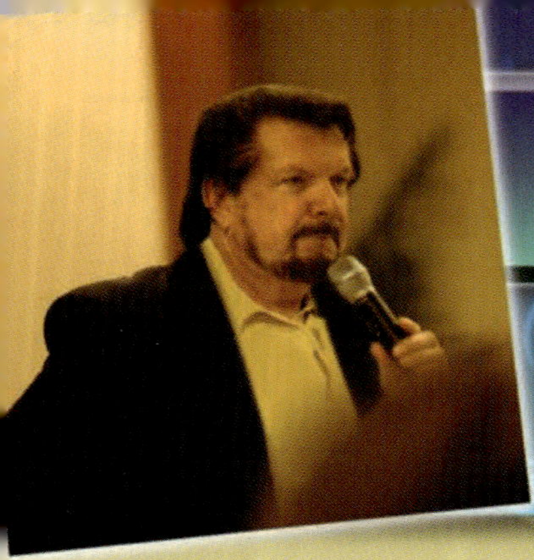

60

Don't Stare...
At The Wall In Front of You.
Circle...
Until You Find "The Door."

61 My "Tweets"...Are My *Thoughts*.
Not My Biography. :)

62 ENDURANCE...
Should Be A Season...Not Your
Lifestyle.
(Re-Visit Your Decision Skills.)

63 TOUGH-TALK:
Somebody Has Invested...In You.
What Has Been Their Return/
Profit..?
Answer.
Honestly.

64 REGRET Is...The First Proof You
Made A *Discovery.*

65 ANYTHING *Unsought*...
Remains *Unfound.*
Think.

66 Liars...*Distrust* Truth.

67 PALACE-TALK:
Guests...Visit.
Servants...*Stay.*

www.twitter.com/DrMikeMurdock

Investment

68

Invest Where You See Reward.

69 *A*fter 1,000 Satanic Attempts To *Kill*
You~Yet, YOU ARE STILL ALIVE.
GOD Is...Protecting AN INVESTMENT
In You.
Find It.

70 *S*ome Invest...In An Experience.
Some Invest...In A *Lifestyle.*
The Difference Is Profound.

71 *I*nvestment...Reveals *Interest.*

72 *T*Relentlessly *Evaluate*...
Profit From Every Single Investment.
~Time
~$$
~Energy
~Advice
It Is Startling.

73 *J*OY Is...The *Return* On
An Investment.

74 *W*HOSE Problems...Matter The *Most*
To You?
What Is The *Proof*...That You Care?
What Has Been Your Investment...
To *Solve* Them?

75

Marriage Is The Seed For Unexpected Wisdom.

76 EVERY RELATIONSHIP...
Has A Cost...Energy...Time...Focus.
Sometimes, The Cost *Exceeds*
The Pleasure.
EVERY PLEASURE...Has A *Price*.

77 SELF-ABSORPTION Is...
The *Enemy* of Relationship.
Not Mere Attitude;
It Is A Philosophy Toward Life.
Self-Worship.

78 ADMIRATION Is...
The Seed For *Relationship*.

79 RELATIONSHIP-KILLER:
~When You *Demand* From Someone...
Something They Do *Not* Possess.
(Time-$$-Love-Romance-Servitude)

80 Think-Twice-Before-MARRIAGE:
~If They Are *Uncomfortable*
In The Presence of God.
~If They *Never* Ask Quality Questions
About Your Assignment.

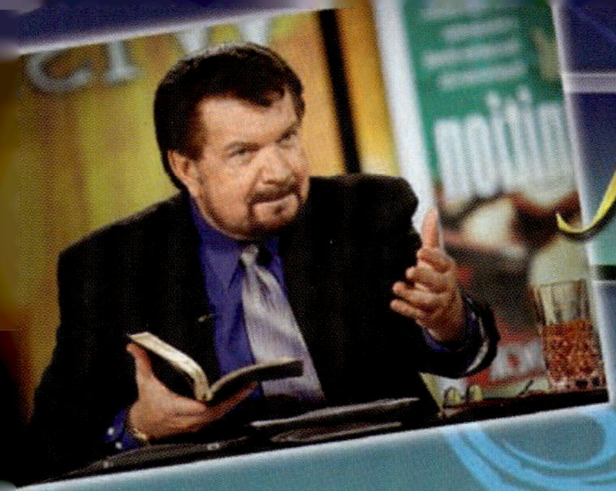

81

Mystery-of-The-Gospel: Something Used...Can Be Exchanged For Something "New." Something Dirty...Can Be Exchanged For Something "Pure."

82 *T*hose *Unwilling* To Come Hear You Teach *Disqualify* Themselves For *Private* Counseling.

83 *P*rayer For Pastors…
"Father, Keep Us Focused/Bold/ Kind…As We Pour Your *Healing* Wisdom Into *Wounded* Hearts of Our People."

84 *P*rayer For Pastors…
"Father, As We Sow Our Persuasions
~Enable Us To FOCUS On The Crushed…Not Critics, Reachers…Not Rebels."

85 *A* Pastor's Life…
"Pastor, I Did Not Go To Church Yesterday; God Told Me To Stay Home, So He Could Talk To Me." Growth?

86 *3* Good Decisions…
1. *Train* Team Via Personal DVD's.
2. *Replace* Disloyalty Swiftly/Quietly.
3. *Identify* Your "Elisha."

Opportunity

87

*O*PPORTUNITY Is...
*Simply An Invitation To
An Experience.
...Embraced or Ignored.*

88 OPPORTUNITY:
Currency:
...$$
...Credibility
...Integrity
...Knowledge
...Energy
...Time
...Favor
...Cheerfulness
What Are You *Not* Using?

89 *E*verything God Promised Arrived...
Disguised As An Opportunity.

90 *E*very Conversation Is...
An Opportunity To *Build*
Credibility...or *Destroy* It.

91 *T*hose *Dismissive* of My Words...
Have *Lost* The Opportunity
To Live In My Heart.

92 *E*verything You Want...
Has A *Hidden* Path To It.
The Path Is Called...*Opportunity*.

93

*P*LANNING...
Makes Your Future Gloriously Predictable.

Planning

94 God Has Never Sponsored...
A Non-Planner.
Just Planners.
(Ark/Tabernacle/Temple)

95 Every *Divine* Plan Is...Completed
Through *Human* Decisions.

96 SUCCESS Is...Simply Order.
Step 1 Towards Order Is...A *Goal*.
Step 2 Is...A *Plan*.
Step 3 Is...*Divine Approval*.

97 When You *Prepare* For Failure...
It Will *Find* You.

98 SUCCESS:
Picture...The Lifestyle You Desire.
Pursue...Mentorship From Who You
Admire.
Plan...Changes In Your Daily
Success Routine.

99 You Don't Qualify...For Anything
You Are *Unwilling* To Reach For.

100 If *You* Don't Create Your Own
Atmosphere...Someone Else *Will*.

101

$\mathcal{A}$ Protégé Is...
Not Someone Who Should
Learn From You.
A Protégé Is...
Someone Who YEARNS
To Learn From You.

102 *W*hoever Gives *First*...
Creates The *Greatest* Debt.
Nobody-Gets-It.
Master-Secret.

103 *I* Don't Correct...Where I See *Error*.
I Correct...Where I See *Humility*.
(Jesus/Pharisees-Zacchaeus)

104 *I* Don't Correct Where I See...
Disagreement.
I Correct Where I See...A *Learner*.

105 *W*hen You Stopped *Asking*...
You Stopped Learning.
When You Stopped *Learning*...
Your Present *Became* Your
Future.

106 *N*otice...Everything.
Focus...On *One* Thing.

107 *N*ever Ignore An Offense;
It Contains Too Much Information.

108 *M*y-Mistakes...
...Attempting To Teach
A Non-Learner.
Energy Loss.

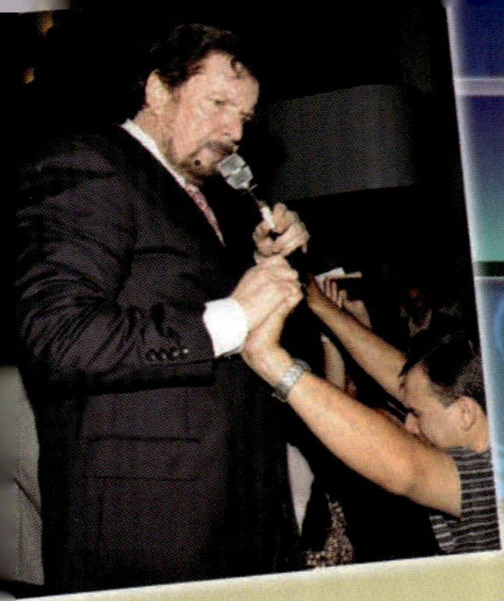

109

The Most Powerful Part
of Any Conversation Is
The Question.

Questions©

110 *W*hat Is *Missing* In Your Life?
A *Nest*...Without Thorns?
A *Voice*...Without Threat?
A *Gift*...Without Motive?
Love...Without Caution?

111 *M*Y QUESTIONS...*Impregnate*
My Environment~
With Explosions of *Revelation* And
Instant *Understanding*.
Penetrates/Dominates.

112 *W*AITING..?
Unasked Questions...
Will NEVER Be Answered.
(Waiting Doesn't Produce Information
Questions Can.)

113 *D*ECISIONS:
When You Have Asked *Enough*
Questions...
Decision-Making Is...*Easy*.
(Questions Are Doors To Knowledge.)

114 *T*he *Fewer* Your QUESTIONS...
The *Longer* Your Journey.
(Pride of The Non-Reacher Is
A Tragedy.)

115

Rejection Is...
When God Disqualifies
Someone You Wouldn't.

116 *R*EJECTION Is...The Divine *Ejection* From Where You Were *Overqualified*.

117 *R*EJECTION Is...Divine *Interruption* To Your Determination To Enter A *Lower* World.

118 *R*EJECTION Is...A Second-Chance That God Is Giving You To Sow In *Quality* Soil.

119 *R*EJECTION Is...A Wise Decision Made By Someone Else.

120 *R*EJECTION Is...Divine Closure of An *Imagined* Door.

121 *R*eaching...Accelerates *Rejection*. Rejection...Accelerates *Freedom*. Freedom Is...The Seed For *Experiences*.

122 *R*EJECTION Is...Not Someone Wanting You Out of Their Life. REJECTION Is...Someone God Wanted Out of *Your* Future.

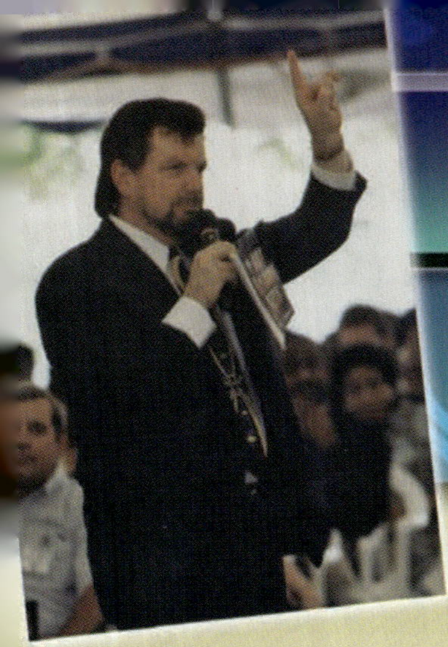

Self-Portrait

123

You Will Always Act Like The Person You Think You Are. (Self-Portrait Decides Self-Conduct.)

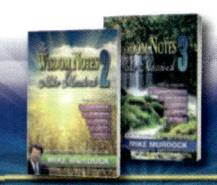

124 *S*omething WITHIN You Is...
Incredibly Valuable.
Find It.

125 *I* Am:
...A Door.
...A Receiver.
I Have Decided...What *Enters* or *Stays.*
I Am A Receiver...of Every Divine Gift.

126 *Y*OU Are A Special Treasure To God.
"Obey My Voice...Keep My Covenant,
THEN...You Shall Be A Special
Treasure To Me."
(Ex. 19:5)

127 *I* Am A Miracle...
Deciding *Where* To Happen Next.
I Will Happen...At 100%.

128 *Y*ou Are *Becoming*...
Whatever You *Admire.*
(Elisha/Elijah)

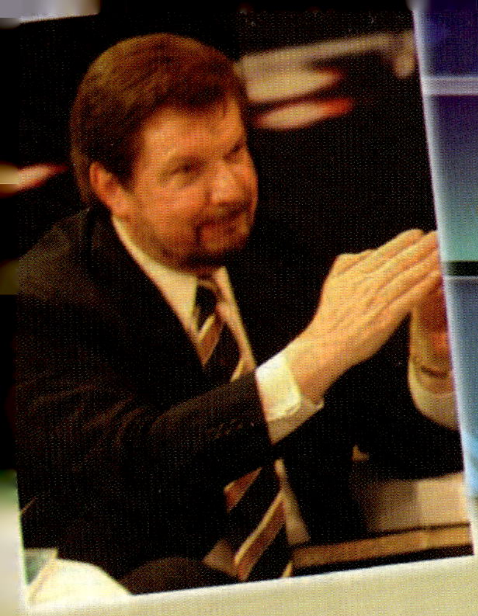

129

If Adam Was Complete...
Eve Was Unnecessary.

130 Predators...Have More Than One Prey.
Remember.

131 What You Are Refusing To Seek...
You Will *Never* Find.
(Jesus/A.S.K./Ask/Seek/Knock)

132 Waiting Is...Not *Always* Proof of Patience.
Waiting Is...Often Proof of *Pride.*

133 Those Who Cannot Discern Your Heart...Will Never Discern You.
Never. Never. *Never.*

134 Disinterest Is...Divine *Protection.*

135 Since My Presence Did Not *Improve* You...I Will *Remove* It.

136 If You Need *More* Than I Am Offering...
You Need What I Do Not Have.

137 The-Right-One...Does Not Happen Until The "Game" Becomes Your...
QUEST.

Sponsor 65

Special Thanks To These Dear Partners Who
Sponsored This Volume...

Laura Allen
Sonia Alma
Diana Amewowor
Kenneth R. Anthony
Patricia L. Austin
Rosalia Beltran-Esquilin
Wilma J. Bennett
Prophetess Magda Beshara
Drs. Jesse and Ada Bullock
Marlena Burton
Rev. Robert G. Cates
Friedel Clarkson
Rita Dempsey
Jeannie Dodge
Esthela Dominguez
Felecia Duson
Lori Ferguson
Christopher E. Fierstein
Marianne Forester
Esther Gall
Mr. & Mrs. Atul Ghelani
Maggie Griffin
Jan Harned
Edith P. Harrison
Rev. Melanie Hart
Judy Hartley
Pamela A. Hoeft
Mr. & Mrs. Robert Hoppes &
Mary Hoppes
Anthony F. Johnson
Mr. & Mrs. Robert Johnson
Wayne R. Jones
Mr. & Mrs. Robert Korpi

Yvette Kuiper
Prophetess Brenda J. Lamb
Ammy G. Lira
Roxanne Mangal
Anesta McDonald
Ps. Wayne L. McKean
Sinder C. Miller
Carlina Mora
Dorothy Murphy
Paul Nyamweya
Adrianna Onwawoma
Evangelist Terri Padilla
Mr. & Mrs. Larry Payne
Mildred Polk
Yelena Primachenko
Lolita T. Quinn
Ruth Redfern
Dr. Henretta M. Reese
Pamela Rikke
Gloria J. Rose
Brenda Segura
Santosh Sherpe
Michelle L. Shirley
Martha Sierra
Melanie Simmons
Bonnie Skeen
Ps. Lynnell Strauss
Dian J. Thomas
Patsy Walker
Ps. & Mrs. Timothy Walker
Gail L. Wescott
Dewayne B. Williams
Shirley Wolff

DECISION

Will You Accept Jesus As Your Personal Savior Today?

The Bible says, "That if thou shalt confess with thy mouth the Lord Jesus, and shalt believe in thine heart that God hath raised Him from the dead, thou shalt be saved," (Romans 10:9).

Pray this prayer from your heart today!

"Dear Jesus, I believe that You died for me and rose again on the third day. I confess I am a sinner...I need Your love and forgiveness...Come into my heart. Forgive my sins. I receive Your eternal life. Confirm Your love by giving me peace, joy and supernatural love for others. Amen."

DR. MIKE MURDOCK

is in tremendous demand as one of the most dynamic speakers in America today.

More than 17,000 audiences in over 100 countries have attended his Schools of Wisdom and conferences. Hundreds of invitations come to him from churches, colleges and business corporations. He is a noted author of over 300 books, including the best sellers, *The Leadership Secrets of Jesus* and *Secrets of the Richest Man Who Ever Lived.* Thousands view his weekly television program, *Wisdom Keys with Mike Murdock.* Many attend his Schools of Wisdom that he hosts in many cities of America.

☐ Yes, Mike, I made a decision to accept Christ as my personal Savior today. Please send me my free gift of your book, *31 Keys to a New Beginning* to help me with my new life in Christ.

NAME _____ BIRTHDAY _____

ADDRESS _____

CITY _____ STATE ____ ZIP _____

PHONE _____ E-MAIL _____ DFC

Mail to: **The Wisdom Center** · 4051 Denton Hwy. · Ft. Worth, TX 76117
1-817-759-BOOK · 1-817-759-2665 · 1-817-759-0300
MikeMurdockBooks.com

47

JOIN THE
Wisdom Key 3000
TODAY!

Thank You For Joining
The Wisdom Key 3000
Pursuing, Proclaiming And Publishing The Word

Will You Become My Ministry Partner In The Work of God?

Dear Friend,

God has connected us!

I have asked The Holy Spirit for 3000 Special Partners who will plant a monthly Seed of $58.00 to help me bring the Gospel around the world. (58 represents 58 kinds of blessings in the Bible.)

Will you become my monthly Faith Partner in The Wisdom Key 3000? Your monthly Seed of $58.00 is so powerful in helping heal broken lives. When you sow into the work of God, 4 Miracle Harvests are guaranteed in Scripture, Isaiah 58...

▶ Uncommon <u>Health</u> (Isaiah 58)
▶ Uncommon <u>Wisdom</u> For <u>Decision-Making</u> (Isaiah 58)
▶ Uncommon <u>Financial Favor</u> (Isaiah 58)
▶ Uncommon <u>Family Restoration</u> (Isaiah 58)

Your Faith Partner,

Mike Murdock

P.S. Please clip the coupon attached and return it to me today, so I can rush the Wisdom Key Partnership Pak to you...or call me at 1-817-759-0300.   PP-03

THE Covenant OF Fifty-Eight Blessings

101 WISDOM KEYS

The Blessing BIBLE

THE CRAZIEST instruction GOD EVER GAVE ME
The Personal Testimony That Has Unlocked Miracles For Millions

WISDOM KEY 3000 PARTNERSHIP SEED BOOK

365 Wisdom Key Scriptures on The Word of God

MIKE MURDOCK

☐ *Yes, Mike, I want to join The Wisdom Key 3000.*
Please rush The Wisdom Key Partnership Pak to me today!
☐ *Enclosed is my first monthly Seed-Faith Promise of:*
☐ *$58* ☐ *Other $_____.*

☐ CHECK   ☐ MONEY ORDER   ☐ AMEX   ☐ DISCOVER   ☐ MASTERCARD   ☐ VISA

Credit Card # _____ Exp. ____ / ____

Signature _____

Name _____ Birth Date ____ / ____

Address _____

City _____ State _____ Zip _____

Phone _____ E-Mail _____

Your Seed-Faith Offerings are used to support The Wisdom Center, and all of its programs. The Wisdom Center reserves the right to redirect funds as needed in order to carry out our charitable purpose. In the event The Wisdom Center receives more funds for the project than needed, the excess will be used for another worthy outreach. (Your transactions may be electronically deposited.)

WK3000

1-817-759-BOOK
1-817-759-2665
1-817-759-0300

— *You Will Love Our Website..!*
MikeMurdockBooks.com